Thriving with
Sensory Processing Differences

OUT-OF-SYNC

success stories

Carol Stock Kranowitz, MA

Author of *The Out-of-Sync Child*

Out-of-Sync Success Stories

817-303-1516
www.sensoryworld.com

ISBN: 978-1-963367-29-4

Contents

Stories about Individuals with Extrasensory Grace
1

Stories about Individuals with Deep Self-Awareness
23

Stories about Individuals with Leadership
47

Stories about Individuals with Artistic & Technological Creativity
63

Stories about Individuals with Fix-It-Ability
77

⋆★ **Preface** ★⋆

A common condition known today as sensory processing differences (SPD) came to my attention in 1986. For almost four decades, I have learned, written, and spoken about SPD and how certain people respond in unusual ways to ordinary sensory stimuli.

This book celebrates fourteen "out-of-sync" individuals. Over the past twenty-five years, their stories have been published in *Autism Digest* (also called *Autism Asperger's Sensory Digest*), *Psychology Today*, and *Child Care Information Exchange*.

These individuals taught me how SPD affects their learning and behavior; what kind of support they need from parents, teachers, and professionals; and how their sensory differences can become sensational assets.

For example, Tommy reluctantly came to the preschool in Washington, DC, where I was the music and movement teacher. Participating in circle time, swinging on the playground, and smearing finger paint were some of the fear-and-tear-producing activities that overwhelmed this little boy.

The good news is that Tommy learned to manage preschool. With occupational therapy and a sensory-rich home life, he became an engaged student. Even more astonishing was his evolution into an amazingly empathetic friend. Quicker than the grown-ups, he could sniff out sensory challenges and anxiety in other little kids. He just knew how to comfort children who needed extra understanding, time, and assurance.

Tommy was the first of many extraordinary individuals I have met who exhibit what I call *extrasensory grace.* His sensory challenges did not disable him; rather, they enabled him to reach out and help others. Nobody taught him how; this gift was all his own.

In this book, Tommy and thirteen other individuals remind us that sensory processing differences are on a continuum. Sensory differences certainly can be limiting—and certainly can be invigorating and inspiring as well.

This collection of stories includes five sections:

1. Extrasensory grace
2. Self-awareness
3. Leadership
4. Artistic and technological creativity
5. Fix-it-ability

These categories overlap, of course. For instance, Jake has extrasensory grace and fix-it-ability, Jeff has outstanding self-awareness and shows artistic creativity, and so forth.

As you read the stories, perhaps you will see yourself in one or more of these highly successful people.

I am in debt to, and in awe of, each individual in this book.

Carol Stock Kranowitz, MA
Bethesda, Maryland
September 2025

stories about Individuals with Extrasensory Grace

Sensory processing differences can be strengthening. All the individuals in this book have developed extraordinary skills in spite of—or because of—having SPD.

The stories of Tommy, Jake, Caitlin, and Sadie are in this section because they exemplify a quality I have termed *extrasensory grace*.

Extrasensory grace: The intrinsic, elegant, spirited, especially gifted talent or quality that comes from within. Extrasensory grace arrives when individuals with SPD learn to accept their limitations, love their quirky selves, discover what they are meant to do, and resolve to make a difference in the world. They are generous-hearted, can-do people, focusing on what is positive and possible.

★★ Tommy's ★★

EXTRASENSORY
Grace

(Originally published in *Autism Digest*, May-July 2019.
Tommy's last name is not used in order to protect his privacy.)

The real Tommy, who was the model for Tactile Tommy in *The Out-of-Sync Child*, resisted coming to preschool. Wearing a perpetual frown, he clung to his mother and wanted nothing to do with an unpredictable troupe of three-year-olds.

Tommy's teachers gently pried him out of his car seat and encouraged him to participate just a little bit in the morning program of playground activities, art projects, and sing-a-longs. Hypervigilant, with his eyes darting in all directions and his back glued to the wall, during the first week of school, he sobbed for three hours. The second week, two hours. The third week, sporadically. After a month to warm up to the idea of becoming a schoolboy, he began to show some interest in his surroundings.

Identifying and Addressing Tommy's SPD

When he came to us, Tommy had not yet been identified with sensory processing differences (SPD), but it was evident that he was highly over-responsive to tactile, auditory, and vestibular sensations. He had come to the right place, because all teachers at St. Columba's Nursery School in Washington, DC, support kids with SPD and other developmental differences.

We observed that he seemed bewildered, as if he didn't know how to play or what to do. His feet never left the ground. He avoided the sandbox and finger paints. He moaned at snack time because the crackers and apples were intolerable.

Tommy's Attunement

However, Tommy had other talents. He loved puzzles and story time. He had amazing verbal skills. And, while he was not tuned into marching and tiptoeing games, he was extraordinarily attuned to other children's emotions. When one whimpered after stumbling on the playground, Tommy whimpered too. When another yelled because someone knocked over his block tower, Tommy yelled too. When another child laughed, Tommy gravely paid attention. We hoped one day to see him laugh too—or at least smile.

OT-SI Benefits

In February of his first year at school, with an occupational therapist consultant, I screened Tommy and all the other three-year-olds for SPD. The screening indicated that he would benefit from occupational therapy using sensory integration techniques (OT-SI). His parents were willing to try anything to help their little boy, so Tommy began therapy and, inch by inch, he began to enjoy school.

As he grew more confident in the "occupation" of childhood, Tommy found two friends, both with identified special needs. Like Tommy, they were more verbal and less active than their classmates.

One was Gabe, who had spina bifida. Gabe wore leg braces to stabilize him when he stood and sat. His forte was building forts with wooden unit blocks, and Tommy began to like this construction work. When Gabe needed a particular block that was out of reach, Tommy obligingly got it for his friend. Tommy told his mother, "Gabe can't get up to reach things. He needs me."

Bunny Love

Another friend was Barbara, a blind girl who introduced Tommy to the joys of stroking the bunny, Poppy. The teacher would lift Poppy from his cage and place him in a rubber bin. Tommy (formerly the boy who could not tolerate being close to another child) and Barbara sat snugly side by side, the bin straddling their legs, petting Poppy.

One day, Poppy pooped in the bin. Tommy had never seen anything like it. Disgusted by the sight and scent, he pinched his nose and hollered, "Oh no! What happened?" Barbara said, "Ooooh,

I know what happened. Poppy pooped!" Tommy told the teacher, "Barbara's eyes don't work, but her nose sure does!"

The school year ended, and the teachers and Tommy's parents agreed that Tommy had made great strides, especially with social and sensory-motor skills. And there was something else—something ineffable. This little boy, so oversensitive to the world around him, was developing an exquisite sensitivity to others' emotions and differing abilities.

September came. Now Tommy, Gabe, and Barbara were "big kids" in the four-year-olds' wing of the school building. Tommy greeted his friends with a hug—a tactile move that would have been unlikely a year ago.

At the end of the first morning, everyone was outside on the playground. Three-year-olds played on one side, and four-year-olds played on the other, separated by a chain-link fence. Tommy and his friends sat on a gym mat, chatting and stroking Poppy, whom they had renamed Poopy.

"I Knew What to Do"

Just then, on the three-year-olds' side of the fence, a child began to cry. I watched as Tommy alerted to the sound, stood up, and approached her. He said something. She nodded. He pressed his forehead against the chain links and stuck his fingers through.

The girl's sobs subsided. Through the chain links, her little hands and forehead met Tommy's. They stood there, connected, for a magical moment. The world stood still.

The girl's teacher came along and coaxed her to join her classmates for a story while they waited for their carpools. Tommy turned back to his friends, his face aglow.

When his mother pulled up in the carpool line, I took him to his car. I was moved by what I had witnessed and wanted to tell her about Tommy's being in sync with someone who was suffering and about his incredible, perfect, generous skill in giving just-right comfort. Many people with SPD have this ability—what I describe as *extrasensory grace* in *The Out-of-Sync Child Grows Up*—but I had never witnessed it in someone so young.

I didn't need to say a word. Tommy, smiling broadly, clambered into his car seat. He said, "Mommy, school was so good today! A little girl was sad, and I knew what to do."

2025 Author's Note: Tommy attended St. Columba's Nursery School in Washington, DC, in the 1980s. I have lost touch with his family.

BECAUSE of

⋆⋆★ Jake ★⋆⋆

(Originally published in *Autism Asperger's Sensory Digest*, February-April 2020.)

Jake Cassell flew into my arms when we met. He wriggled onto my lap, jiggled my earrings, and giggled with delight. At four, he wasn't speaking much, but we needed no words to communicate. After leaving his home—where I had gone to consult his mother, Jennifer, my website designer—I felt happy all day.

That was Jake's effect on everybody. Like many others with autism and sensory issues, he exhibited extrasensory grace, a certain quality that connected him to people. You'd meet him, you'd instantly be in sync, and later, as you went about your daily doings, you'd feel his nearness, like having an angel on your shoulder.

A few seasons ago, after a hiatus of several years, we met again at his house. Jake enfolded me in a hug, saying, "Haven't seen you in a while!"

"Do you remember me, Jake?"

"Sure! You're special!"

How did he remember me? He just did. To him, everyone was special and memorable.

The Giver

Jennifer recounts going to church with Jake when he was small. As the family settled into their seats, Jake reached back to give his hand to a woman in the pew behind them. She gripped his little hand, inhaled, exhaled, and began to sob. "We didn't know her or her story. But Jake knew. He just knew," Jennifer says.

Jake grew tall and handsome and, thanks to years of physical therapy and occupational therapy, well-coordinated. He excelled at biking, rock climbing, and swimming, giving these activities his all.

One summer afternoon, seventeen-year-old Jake set out on his bicycle to the YMCA swimming pool. He rode on the sidewalk, as usual, because riding in the busy street was hazardous. Jake swerved to avoid a row of trash cans, lost control of his bike, and toppled into the street. A driver couldn't avoid hitting him. The next morning, Jake died.

Because of Jake's death, many things have happened. For example, the Maryland Department of Transportation installed three miles of bicycle lanes to protect pedestrians and bikers along this dangerous stretch of road. The family established the Jake Cassell Scholarship Fund at the Diener School, where Jake attended elementary school, to benefit autistic children whose families cannot afford the tuition. Another fund is the Jake Cassell Fund for Special Needs, which empowers grassroots organizations that serve children and young adults with developmental differences in underserved communities through grants and partnerships.

The Role Model

Because of Jake's life, even more good things happened. He became a role model for other youngsters within the special needs community in dancing, theater, bocce, softball, and other endeavors. Deeply religious and passionate about worship and service, he loved participating with his friends and pastor at his church's Rock Youth Ministry. He helped lead a Vacation Bible School in the Dominican Republic and encouraged his teammates on the bocce and softball teams at Winston Churchill High School to exert themselves and play their best.

Jake also loved being a Boy Scout. He inspired his fellow Scouts to plan carefully for campouts and to be task-oriented in the merit badge system. When he died, he was one rank shy of Eagle Scout, which he anticipated achieving at the end of the summer.

The Inventor, Fixer, Artist, and Musician

What would the world be like without people like Jake? Temple Grandin says, "The world needs people with autism to invent things, fix things, and make art and music." Because he had autism and sensory differences, Jake did all these things sensationally.

- **Invent things:** (Inventors with autism include Alan Turing, father of computer science and artificial intelligence; Vernon Smith, inventor of experimental economics; and Satoshi Tajiri, creator of Pokémon.) In the summer before he died, Jake was developing a blueprint to include blue LED lights on every airplane, since he found these to be soothing. His goal was to incorporate comfortable lighting in the cabins and on the TVs to make airplanes more pleasant for every traveler. He planned to submit his invention to Boeing when the drawing that was spread across the dining room table was completed.

- **Fix things:** (Fixers with autism include Temple Grandin, whose humane animal handling systems improve the welfare of livestock; John Elder Robison, an advocate for autism-related policies and research; and Greta Thunberg, climate activist and *TIME* magazine's 2019 Person of the Year.) Noticing that his high school's sports teams lacked an active mascot, Jake volunteered to don the Bulldog costume with the fierce headpiece. The fact that it was smelly and confining did not bother him a bit. Jake not only relished but also revolutionized this physically uncomfortable and potentially embarrassing role. His goal was not to intimidate the opponents, but to inspire the home teams. In one year, he attended more than fifty athletic games!

Jake the Bulldog in his fierce costume, at Winston Churchill High School in Potomac, Maryland

Because of his success in building school spirit, the principal, Brandice Heckert, and the PTA raised funds to purchase a new Bulldog costume with a smiling face to match Jake's happy personality. She intended to give it to him in September, saying, "He was so excited about it. He deserved it." The cheerful mascot uniform is named "Jake."

The new, cheerful Jake the Bulldog, with "In loving memory of Jake Cassell" on the back

- Make art: (Artists with autism include Michelangelo, Andy Warhol, and Stephen Wiltshire, who draws complicated cityscapes after one quick glance.) Jake's autistic, artistic eye for innovative visual design developed as he grew. Mike Schechter, Jake's Cub Scout leader, describes a weird, unappetizing cake that Jake created for a baking project. It was a sheet cake covered with blue sprinkles and Tootsie Rolls. Mr. Schechter asked Jake what his idea was and recalls, "He fell over laughing. The cake was decorated to look like a cat litter box!" When the other Cub Scouts understood his zany joke, they devoured the cake. In the weeks prior to his accident, Jake was designing, with phenomenal detail, a wooden walkway (called a *puncheon*) from which to observe a natural wetland at Patuxent River State Park as his Eagle Scout project. His Boy Scout Troop 233 completed the project in his memory.
- Make music: (Musicians with autism include singer, guitarist, songwriter, and actress Courtney Love; singer Susan Boyle, a winner on *Britain's Got Talent*; and Wolfgang Amadeus Mozart.) As a musician, Jake sang at church events and local teenage karaoke spots, specializing in songs such as "Lean on Me," "Carry Me Away," and countless worship songs. With his extrasensory in-tune-ness, intuition, and natural rhythm, he accompanied other performers on the bongo drums and got everyone on their toes, singing, clapping, and moving in sync.

Because of autism—not in spite of it—Jake made things happen. With extrasensory grace, love, and joy, helping everyone do better was his mission.

"You can do this," he would say, pumping his fist. "Bring it home. Do it!"

Because of Jake, we are doing our best.

Jacob Brian Cassell
October 10, 2001–August 1, 2019

★★ Caitlin Folliard ★★

JUMPS for Joy

(Originally published in *Autism Digest* in 2025.)

s a little girl, Caitlin Folliard always wanted to get her hands on slime, the icky, sticky, gloopy substance made from glue, water, and borax that children can mold and stretch. This kind of intensely messy play was definitely OK.

Certain other touch experiences, however, were intolerable. (Sensory processing differences are rife with such inconsistencies.) For instance, Caitlin had eating issues around the textures of food. Clothes were often uncomfortable, and seams in socks were particularly bothersome, so she wore them inside out. Rough textures, like the bristles on her toothbrush and random objects that were not completely smooth, were absolutely not OK.

Additional vestibular and proprioceptive challenges affected her functioning in daily life. Her balance was off-kilter, her posture sagged, and her fine-motor skills lagged. She had dysgraphia, a sensory-based motor difficulty with handwriting.

> **Dysgraphia ("difficulty" plus "writing"):** A disability in transcription, which involves handwriting, typing, and spelling. Sensations of touch, sight, and movement are not well integrated, resulting in poor fine-motor coordination. About 40 percent of children with SPD have dysgraphia. The child may awkwardly grip the pencil, write illegibly, mumble while writing, omit words, make grammatical mistakes, and have problems organizing and expressing thoughts on the page, even when those thoughts are brilliant.

In middle school, misophonia developed into a big problem for her as well. This condition worsened during COVID. Caitlin said about the time during which her school was closed, "I hid in my bedroom. But I could still hear my brother typing on his computer and my mother's office chair squeaking, many floors away from my room."

> **Misophonia ("hatred" plus "sound"):** The extreme dislike of certain bodily sounds such as chewing, swallowing, sniffling, throat clearing, and foot tapping, and of environmental sounds such as clicking pens and typing, or traffic and construction. Specific sounds, called trigger sounds, cause intense emotions, including anxiety, disgust, or rage. Misophonia is a type of auditory overresponsivity that often co-occurs with SPD.

Life-Changing Treatment

Fortunately, by then, Caitlin was receiving life-changing occupational therapy using a sensory integration approach (OT-SI) with Kristen Masci, MS, OTR/L, at the Skills on the Hill therapy clinic in Arlington, Virginia. Kristen used a brushing technique on Caitlin's arms and legs to reduce her over-responsivity to tactile sensations.

Caitlin worked with beads and other small objects to improve her fine-motor skills and eye-hand coordination. She spun on tire swings, wriggled through nets, and scaled climbing walls to improve her postural responses, motor coordination, and stamina. She loved "riding" bolsters suspended from the ceiling.

Occupational therapy continued to help Caitlin as she grew and her sensory challenges evolved. She really liked her therapist. She recalls an assignment in third grade to research and write about an interesting occupation, and interviewing Kristen about her work seemed easy enough to do. In the process, Caitlin realized that the field of OT was really cool!

Another life-changing experience—not only for Caitlin, but also for the whole family—was starting to attend McLean School in Potomac, Maryland, in fifth grade. The school uses an abilities approach that begins with the students' gifts and teaches them the way they learn. The school specializes in helping children with dyslexia, dysgraphia, ADHD, anxiety, and other learning issues. The teachers' treatment included accommodations such as speech-to-text technology and audiobooks that helped Caitlin immensely.

Joyful Horseback Riding

Along with OT-SI and the right school, another experience has profoundly shaped Caitlin's development. When she was nine, she first attended Camp Friendship in the Blue Ridge Mountains, where campers ride horses for half of each day. Caitlin was in heaven. She discovered that every aspect of the intense sensory experiences of riding and wrangling horses was totally OK.

At a barn near her home, she shows her talent for riding horses competitively. She often wins blue ribbons as an equestrienne in the Hunter Horse category, where rider and horse are judged for how perfectly in sync they move while jumping. For this skill, "Good core balance is required," Caitlin says. "My back is not my strong suit, and riding strengthens my balance. Not only that, but I've noticed the more I ride, the less my misophonia bothers me. I'm concentrating on moving and jumping together with my horse. Movement can drown out the sounds."

Caitlin jumps not only on horses but also on her own two feet playing defense on her high school basketball team. "Maybe I'm a little aggressive on the court, but I'm better at defense than offense. My shooting's not the best because my eye-hand coordination still isn't that great, but my jumping is good. I also play center back in soccer, another defense position." She adds, "I like to run fast."

What's next? In summertime at equestrian camp, Caitlin works as the in-barn leader with children ages six through thirteen. She oversees their horse-related arts and crafts and unmounted games and helps them learn how to feed the horses and care for their saddles, bits, reins, and countless other pieces of riding equipment.

Goal to Become an OT

And after that? Smiling hugely, Caitlin says, "Ever since I was eight, I have wanted to be an OT. I understand what it feels like to have SPD. I know what helps. And I like working with kids. I like them a lot better than grown-ups."

When asked what Caitlin would like the world to know about her, she replies, "Lots of people don't realize I'm as smart as I am. While misophonia is a lot to deal with, I can hear things other people cannot hear. I have almost perfect auditory working memory too.

"Yes, I have dysgraphia, and I'm a slow reader, but with accommodations, I can be just as competitive in the classroom as the next

> **Auditory working memory:** The mental process of temporarily remembering and using information you hear in order to understand what is said, learn new facts, plan and reason, follow instructions, and solve problems.

person. I'm taking AP biology now and plan to take AP psychology when I'm a senior. And I'm smarter than I show."

Caitlin exemplifies extrasensory grace. She is in tune with animals and other children with differences. She is aware of her challenges and appreciates her strengths. She is ready to show the world what she can do. Indeed, Caitlin has a lot to show.

Caitlin and her horse Anton

stories about Individuals with Deep Self-Awareness

It goes without saying that most of the individuals in this book are self-aware of their differences, both limiting and empowering. Sadie, Luke, and Jeff particularly focus on self-reflection and understanding their personal challenges.

Sadie Friedman

TOUCHES the World

(Originally published in *Autism Digest*, November 2024-January 2025)

Sadie Friedman and Ethan the Rabbit

t's just easier to be with animals," says Sadie Friedman. As we settle down for a Zoom chat, she hoists her snow-white therapy animal, Ethan, onto her lap. She cuddles and strokes this enormous rabbit, the size of a cocker spaniel, and says, "Animals don't expect you to do small talk."

While small talk with humans can be a big challenge, Sadie has always communicated easily with animals, birds, reptiles, and bugs. She grew up collecting critters while she explored the woods and waded in creeks near her Maryland home. She remembers being a preschooler in search of seventeen-year cicadas during the emergence of Brood X in 2004.

Chilling with a Chipmunk

She also recalls an elementary-school field trip to Washington's National Zoo. "We were lined up outside the gorilla house, just chilling in one spot," she says. "I saw a chipmunk near the railing. It was just chilling too. I leaned down and petted him. He sat there and let me pet him."

Sadie's ability to be a chipmunk whisperer—her extrasensory grace—is one of her noteworthy differences. Indeed, her teacher was so impressed with the chipmunk incident that he sent her parents a note praising her special gift.

Meanwhile, autism, SPD, and dyslexia hindered Sadie's academic success. Her bugaboos included certain sounds and textures that were as uncomfortable as they were unavoidable. This smart girl disliked school and was not college bound.

One day, in the car on the way to high school, she told her mother, Laurie, "I can't, I can't, I just can't do it."

The Car Wash (and Other Therapy)

Laurie got it. She turned the car around and drove straight to the car wash. They sat inside the car and got a vigorous vestibular, proprioceptive, visual, and auditory workout. Then they went to the park for a nature walk and bumped into a therapist friend who gave Sadie a little craniosacral therapy. The friend had a Bernese mountain dog with her, which Sadie sat with and petted for a while.

Craniosacral therapy (CST): An alternative treatment using a gentle touch to manipulate the cranium or skull, the pelvis, and the spine to treat various issues. Developed in the 1970s by John Upledger, a doctor of osteopathy, CST can make significant improvements in individuals with SPD when used in conjunction with OT-SI.

Guess what? This spontaneous, multi-part therapeutic program included the alerting, organizing, and calming ingredients that were just right for that girl on that morning. This was an example of great collaboration: Sadie could express what her challenge was, her mother could recognize and cope with Sadie's sensory needs, the therapist could practice her art and science on the spot, and the dog could provide the final touch of soothing sensory input.

Being Misunderstood

Learning at school has been hard, but teaching others is something Sadie does well. She has found satisfaction working for Montgomery County Parks as a shadow for kids with special needs. "I'm OK with most children," she says. "I'm entering adulthood and have a better understanding. "Kids with special needs see the world so differently. To other people, they can seem scary if they're dysregulated and their behavior is odd. I know what that's like."

She muses, "A lot of scary animals are misunderstood. Arthropods, like scorpions and tarantulas, are pretty cool. They aren't really aggressive. They only sting or bite when they are scared themselves. The first thing a tarantula does when it's scared is to kick hairs off its thorax. That's the big round part that includes the abdomen and butt. The hairs are itchy. Predators don't like the itchy feeling and back away."

Sadie has often cradled tarantulas in her hand. The critters are unafraid and don't kick hairs. Sadie is calm too. On the other hand, she finds that touching a particular book cover may give her the creeps. Such are tactile differences!

Today, Sadie strokes Ethan's long ears and says thoughtfully, "Tarantulas are like people with autism. When there are too many demands, we may seem scary, but we just want to flick our hairs and run away—no real damage done!"

Caring for Animals

Now twenty-three, Sadie has found her niche as a trainee at Petco, a major pet supply chain. She enjoys her apprenticeship in the art of dog grooming while she learns skills such as handling skittish puppies, determining how high an animal's quick is before clipping its nails, and giving pattern haircuts, including the skirt cut for schnauzers and the lamb cut for poodles. At the completion of her training, she will have a license, a job, and a future.

Finding her niche has changed Sadie's life. The Petco training program may be a good fit for many animal lovers like her. "We are just people," she says. "Dyslexia and ASD—they're just a trait that people have. Sure, I'm going to be slow sometimes. I need a minute to process information, to check and recheck directions. But you know what? My teacher seems happy to have me double-check how to use a nail clipper!"

In answer to a question about life goals, Sadie says, "I have a fantasy to start my own business, my own wildlife facility. I'd like to teach people what to do, say, with an injured squirrel. And to educate people on why pets behave the way they do, how to understand fur and how to get rid of mats, what products to use to care for pets, and especially how to touch them. I'd like to write a mini-guide. I have a lot of things I'm good at and a lot of things I'd like to make happen, and now I know I can do them."

As we end our chat, Sadie eases Ethan the Rabbit off her lap and rises. She has work to do.

Luke

Shares
"A SECRET"

(Originally published in *Autism Digest*, May-July 2022.
To protect his privacy, this boy's name has been changed.)

O vernight camp with classmates? No way! Overwhelming sensory challenges would surely drive twelve-year-old Luke into a state of incoherence and anxiety. Even the *anticipation* of being immersed in nature, with the confusing sounds of warbling birds and babbling brooks ... of sleeping in a tent packed with unpredictable kids ... and of eating not-Mom's food triggered Luke's anxiety.

But Luke didn't want to lose being part of the group.

So his family used a problem-solving method that occupational therapists call *clinical reasoning*. This involves analyzing what is happening around and within the child and then thinking of modifications to help the child become more comfortable in his or her body and environment.

The proactive, preventative approach the family used is called A SECRET, explained below. It was developed by Lucy Jane Miller, PhD, OTR, founder and former director of the STAR Institute. (See her book *Sensational Kids*, as well as another book she co-authored with therapists Lisa Porter and Doreit Bialer, titled, *No Longer A SECRET: Unique Common Sense Strategies for Children with Sensory and Regulation Challenges*.)

Luke, his parents, his OT Lisa Porter, and his teachers worked out a winning compromise. During the day, Luke would do particular physical exercises to get the proprioception and movement his nervous system required. He would think hard and use willful control to stay calm in overstimulating, noisy, woodsy experiences. And at night, he (and his mom) would sleep at a motel.

Overnight camp with classmates? With a few accommodations—you bet!

A Changed Family

Looking back, Luke, now sixteen, says, "I've always been interested in using my brain to influence how I acted. A SECRET gave me a set of sensory tools to use. They were hard to learn at first, but now they're hardwired."

For instance, rules are especially important to Luke; he gets annoyed when people disrespect them. Today, instead of having a meltdown or requesting a break so he can leave the classroom, Luke knows to jump or stretch to get calming input into his muscles and joints. He says, "I don't have to remove myself when something happens in the environment that I can't control. I know how to self-regulate. I know what to do and say."

Luke's mother says, "A SECRET permeated our home culture and changed our parenting. It gave us the power to advocate for our son. One of our angels, his OT, gave us permission to make changes that could be perceived as odd," like the motel arrangement. "It was *epic* for us to learn we were good parents."

Luke's father adds, "The process gave Luke the words to use in triggering situations. And it taught us that parents have the agency to find safety valves for sensory kids who can't measure up to teachers' expectations."

Most importantly, Luke developed a better understanding of his body, his sensory needs, and his emotions. With this growing self-awareness, he could trust himself to make improvements in his own behavior. Rather than shrinking from participation in the world around him, now he could shine.

What A SECRET Means

A SECRET is an acronym for seven elements: attunement, sensation, emotion regulation, culture (customs, habits or routines), relationship, environment, and task. Implementing A SECRET, parents, teachers, children, and teenagers learn to analyze these seven ele-ments in sensory or motor challenges and then come up with ideas that may lead to smoother functioning. A SECRET is not a rigid formula for *what to do*, but a flexible format for *how to think* about manipulating these elements.

First, choose one challenge area, such as getting dressed. Then ask yourselves questions about how to alter a few of the seven ele-ments. These changes may pertain to sensory-motor-based skills that the child struggles with, including self-help skills, fine-motor skills, coordination, or organization. As an example, let's imagine a daughter whose problem is putting on clothes in the morning.

Example of A SECRET

Challenge Area: Getting Dressed

A = Can I improve my *attunement* to my daughter's emotional needs and moods? I won't reason with her or make demands when I see her burrowing into her bed. Instead, I can say, "You look comfortable! Wouldn't it be nice to spend the whole day snug-gled under the covers?" Being empathetic may draw her out.

S = Can I find a fun, feel-good *sensory* strategy? A morning back rub or rolling a therapy ball over her may get input into her skin and muscles that will prime her to get dressed.

E = Can she do something to affect her *emotion regulation* in the moment? Perhaps playing her favorite upbeat music or bright-ening (or dimming) the room lighting would get her in the mood.

C = What could I change about the *culture* or patterns of our family's behavior? (This element focuses on how one does things at home or wherever the challenge occurs; it does *not* refer to the arts or to ethnic customs.) Our custom is to dress before breakfast, but we can change the culture so she can dress afterward.

R = Could I retune our *relationship* to motivate her? Letting her wear what's comfortable and not saying what looks best may help her dress quickly. We could plan a mother-daughter shopping trip on a quiet weekday when she can select new clothes.

E = What in our *environment* could I change? I can install hooks in her closet so she needn't fuss with hangers, or set up labeled bins (T-shirts, Socks, etc.) instead of having a visually confusing jumble in a drawer. A dressing schedule posted on the wall may help, too.

T = Can I add or subtract a *task* to change the situation? She could lay out her clothes the night before or use a visual schedule and check off each item as she goes.

Implementing A SECRET takes a bit of practice, as do all worthwhile and life-changing endeavors. However, it can not only have a major impact on the child but also make school and family life much smoother. For example, parents and teachers at an IEP meeting could collaborate on problem-solving tasks. A proactive problem-solving approach like this is definitely A SECRET to share!

Learn More about A SECRET

To learn about using A SECRET, go to the website of the STAR Institute for Sensory Processing at https://sensoryhealth.org/basic/parent-workshop-series-using-a-secret-to-support-online-learning.

Meanwhile, consider this sample chart with another adult who knows your child well. In the first column, write the problem your child is having, such as "Playing with Brother" or "Math Homework." In other columns, fill in ideas where you can, such as "Do 8 push-ups for proprioception" under "Sensation," or "Put on Mozart" under "Emotion Regulation," or "Play outdoors first; start homework later" under "Culture." Fill in what you can. You need not fill in every column.

Problem-Solving with A SECRET (Sample Chart)

Challenge Area: _____

Attune-ment	Sensation	Emotion regulation	Culture	Relation-ships	Environ-ment	Task

2025 Author's Note: "Luke" is nineteen, living in Oregon, and thriving, thanks to OT-SI, great parenting, and maturity. In regard to his childhood sensory challenges, he says, "I am much more accustomed to the world now. It's incredibly seldom that I find sensory problems are an issue."

His super sensitivity to what he hears, a detriment when he was younger, is now an advantage. He has always been drawn to music and enjoys classes in experimental and/or electronic musical composition.

With his finely tuned auditory skills, he is finding it easy to learn German. His goal is to speak the language fluently and attend law school and practice in Germany.

★ ★ Jeffrey Simonoff ★ ★

From Worrisome Childhood to WONDERFUL Adulthood

(Originally published in *Autism Digest*, February-April 2022.)

Jeffrey at four, with make-believe eyeglasses

Decemeber 2003: My sister-in-law Nomi calls. She is worried about her precious grandson, Jeffrey Simonoff, almost two years old.

During his first year, Jeff has wowed us with his precocious behavior. At six months he began to talk. At eight months, he stood up and ran, skipping the intermediate steps of crawling and walking. With outstanding motor skills, he could climb, pull himself along under the monkey bars, and outshine his little peers on every piece of playground equipment.

But Nomi frets on the telephone. These days Jeffrey is having frequent meltdowns. He has become a fussy eater with poor digestion (due to not-yet-diagnosed celiac disease). He resists baths and getting dressed. He doesn't sleep soundly, so his parents, Melissa and Randy, and siblings, Brynna and Benjamin, don't either. Jeffrey can't play well with other toddlers. He hits. He bites. And recently, he has stopped talking. "He may have a developmental problem," Nomi says. "It's called autism. Have you heard of it?"

A New World

December 2021: "Looking back," Jeffrey's mother Melissa says, "I guess I was in a fog. I remember the pediatrician noticing how Jeff shook his head and rolled his eyes. Also, he banged his head. I said, 'Oh, he does that because he likes the sound.' The doctor said, 'That's unusual behavior ... but I'm not sure it's autism.' I heard that and thought, 'Huh? Where did that idea come from?'

"Things began to add up," Melissa continues. "In his playgroup, Jeffrey didn't respond when his name was called. I thought he might be hard of hearing. At eighteen months, he had a hearing test but wouldn't respond or point to the correct ear, and the audiologist thought he had an attitude problem. Then, after a three-hour psychological evaluation, the psychiatrist advised me that Jeffrey was autistic."

The family was at the threshold of a new world.

Once they got the message, Melissa and Randy (for whom the diagnosis was not a surprise) got to work. They set out to learn everything they could by reading about autism and sensory processing differences, attending conferences, consulting with educators and therapists, and interacting with experienced and supportive families.

Doing Great

At nineteen, Jeffrey is doing great! Living at home, he helps out by cooking dishes such as gluten-free quesadillas and pineapple curry. He delivers meals for DoorDash, using his mother's car until he has saved enough to buy his own. At Pike's Peak Community College, where he's on the dean's list, he studies computer coding, calculus, and physics. ("As for physics," he says, pointing a finger toward the sky, "now, *that's* really something!") He will transfer to the University of Colorado in Colorado Springs as a junior.

In a couple of recent Zoom gatherings, we talked about Jeffrey's path from worrisome childhood to wonderful adulthood. Here are some stories about what he has learned.

Deep Pressure to Get in Sync

Squeezes and tight spaces help Jeffrey get in sync. He likes being under weighted blankets and feeling headphones press against his skull, often without sound. He says, "I like all the things that claustrophobics don't."

As a little boy, his time-in place was his sleeping bag. He would cram it with stuffed animals and then squeeze himself in among them. When he got overexcited or began to stim, his parents would hug him or squeeze his hands. Tactile and proprioceptive input to his skin and body continues to be calming and organizing.

One Mean Teacher and Thirty Kind Classmates

Jeffrey says, "Other kids saw me in a positive or neutral light. Mostly, I wasn't bullied. But in third grade, some of the kids would knock me around. The teacher ignored bullying. She was actually hostile. She took away a Bakugan toy, even though fidgets were in my IEP, and didn't return it until the end of the year. I needed it! I couldn't find the words to tell her. That year I went through a phase when I was at a low point and felt suicidal."

Randy says, "When we saw marks on his body from being bounced against the walls when the teacher wasn't paying attention, we went to school to talk to her. We tried to help her understand his needs, but she was not very responsive ... it was so painful." He swallows. "Jeffrey has learned he must speak up for himself."

Fortunately, most teachers and classmates have been terrific. Melissa says, "When Jeffrey was in sixth grade, we went to a PPT (parent/paraprofessional/teacher) meeting to discuss his IEP. The teacher said, 'Jeffrey doesn't have one advocate in the classroom,' and our hearts sank because we thought things had been going well. Then she said, 'No, not one—he has thirty!' She was a wonderful teacher, and he was surrounded by thirty really kind kids."

Dealing with Criticism

Jeffrey has enjoyed the physically and mentally challenging martial art, tae kwon do. His regular instructor understood when Jeff needed a bathroom break or a drink of water to deal with symptoms of celiac disease.

One day, when Jeff was fifteen, a different teacher refused to permit a break. Hypercritical (and hyposympathetic!), this teacher said, "You always take too long. You fool around in there."

Jeffrey was so angry that he refused to attend classes for several years. Telling me this story, he says, "I was depressed, hollow, not fulfilled. I wanted the physical activity, but this teacher turned me off. I had to learn to ask for help and not just walk away. I'm better at asking now. I'm ready to go back. We are social beings; we need other people."

Custom Drawing

"Drawing helps me calm down. That's how I express myself," Jeffrey says. "I draw with a pencil. Pens ... I don't like pens. Pens have a lot of issues. They open themselves to mistakes, and I can't correct them. I draw animé and manga—Japanese art forms. I want to go to Japan, learn more about the art, and maybe work for Nintendo.

Jeffrey's fulfillment of a request for a custom drawing

"I post my drawings on Reddit." He smiles and points to himself. "It used to be so hard to take criticism. Now, it's OK to put myself out there to be critiqued." In addition, he has been promoting his animé drawings on different forums for the past few years, and he's had several like-minded people ask him for custom drawings that he tries to fulfill.

Being Autistic

Jeff says, "I don't have a big problem with autism." He frowns, concentrating. "I'd say there are just a few small autistic behaviors I have … Here are three."

Jeffrey holds up one finger. "I speak formally. But I don't always get the words out, even though I have always been more mentally mature than other kids. I have apraxia. My problem is word retrieval. It's frustrating when you have ideas but can't say them, and when people don't listen to you."

> **Apraxia:** A neurological disorder making it difficult for an individual to carry out tasks, movements, or verbal responses on demand, although the person understands the request and is willing to comply. Apraxia of speech interferes with moving one's lips or tongue correctly to make appropriate sounds.

He holds up a second finger. "As for my emotional baggage, sometimes I become over-reactive, which I'm not proud of, and sometimes I just don't show any emotion. And it's hard to read other people's emotions."

Melissa gives an example of how Jeffrey is learning to understand emotions. She turns to him and says, "When the dog died and I needed your help to take his body to be cremated, I was so, so upset, but you didn't react at first because I was calm. But later, Jeff, you hugged me and offered to drive us home because you came to understand how much more upset I was than you were. You showed true compassion."

Jeffrey nods, pleased.

Randy says, "How about impulsivity? Tell Aunt Carol about the bear spray."

Jeff laughs and says, "Yes, let's have at it." He holds up a third finger. "I have to think hard about not being impulsive—like the time I pulled the pin on the bear spray canister. You see, it said, 'Pull the pin.' I felt like the instructions were telling me that I must do it. Other kids would know not to do it just because that's what the instructions say. And not in the kitchen, I guess."

Being Human, Being Known

"I think of myself as basically normal. I'm human. I try not to be eccentric. I don't think of myself as being at the top of the heap with my computer skills and art, and I'm not going to blow my horn. Trying to be humble. But I want to ... to somewhat stand out. Not to be a famous celebrity, not like the prime minister of Japan or anything like that, but to have the just-right kind of personality. To make my mark doing something I do well. I would like to be known."

If only Jeffrey's grandmother could see him now!

Jeffrey at twenty-three

2025 Author's Note: In May, Jeffrey received his Bachelor of Innovation in Computer Science from the University of Colorado/Colorado Springs. He was on the dean's list (3.75–3.99 grade point average) and president's list (4.0 grade point average) several times.

He looks forward to a career in computer science and software engineering. He has strong aspirations to design video games and would like to have a side career of accepting artistic commissions and offering website design.

Jeff's drawing of Poseidon, the Greek god of the sea, who is sometimes depicted as a horse

stories about Individuals with Leadership

Because he couldn't walk, Pryce's success in his preschool movement class was unexpected. Because of their early difficulties with talking, Daniel's and Hannah's success in communicating with others was an unpredictable development.

And yet ... Pryce became the choreographer and Daniel became the conductor of their classmates' musical movement activities, while Hannah grew up to be an off-Broadway stage manager.

★★★ Pryce Bevan's ★★★

AWESOME
Moves

(From an article, "Music and Movement Bring Together Children of Differing Abilities," originally published in *Child Care Information Exchange*, May 2000.)

Pryce holding Dog puppet and telling Gingerbread Man, "Woof, I'm going to eat you up!"

ryce, almost five, is bright and beautiful, friendly and fun-loving. He also has spinal muscular atrophy. He is one of about 20 percent of the children with special needs attending the regular preschool program at St. Columba's Nursery School.

Pryce has limited sensory and motor awareness below his hips and thus has little use of his lower body. As a result of extensive and intensive therapy, however, Pryce's upper body is strong. Using a wheelchair, he maneuvers expertly outdoors and indoors.

In my music, movement, and drama room, he excels at singing and rhyming, at seated parachute games and rhythm band activities. He welcomes enacting playlets, such as "The Gingerbread Man." When the farmers and animals run, run, as fast as they can in pursuit of the Gingerbread Man, Pryce joins the chase in his wheelchair. "Watch!" he says. "I can do it myself!"

Music and Movement Activities for All

Pryce is decidedly less enthusiastic about up-and-down activity songs, such as "The Noble Duke of York." He mutters, "I hate that song." Who could blame him?

Still, the musical activities he shuns are often the ones other children love. While inclusion is the name of the game and sensitivity to Pryce's feelings is crucial, the other children have needs too. Balancing the needs of all the children is all-important.

Pryce's classmates are a varied bunch. Several children have excellent motor skills, while others are at various points along the developmental bell curve.

One day the program starts with a quick warm-up game to strengthen the sensory-motor skills of body awareness, motor coordination, flexion and extension, listening, and beat awareness. We sit in a circle, legs in front. The singer on the phonograph record[1]

1. Yes, a phonograph record! This article was written in 2000.

instructs us to raise and lower our feet and wave them in big arcs. Most of us do our best, while Pryce slumps and scowls.

Next, the singer tells us to move our arms, shoulders, and head—up, down, and all around. Pryce can do this. He sits up tall and easily complies with each of these above-the-waist demands.

A Different Idea

Then Pryce says, "I have a different idea. Let's lie on our tummies."

Hey! Cool! We have played this game before, but never on our stomachs. Pryce's compensatory strategy sounds like fun.

We roll onto our stomachs and repeat the activity. Pryce cannot raise his toes, but he has had plenty of tummy time and has phenomenal strength in his torso and neck. He can lift his arms, shoulders, and head high. His agility impresses the other children.

"How do you get your arms so high?" Giorgio asks.

Pleased, Pryce says, "Oh, I'm just really good at that."

Giorgio says, "You're awesome."

Pryce receives the compliment graciously.

More Ideas Follow

Then Giorgio says to me, "Pryce had a good idea. I have a good idea too. Can we do it on our backs?"

Following Giorgio's suggestion, we flip onto our backs and repeat the game, lifting our arms, head, and, when possible, our legs into the air. We discover that when our bodies rest on the floor, resisting gravity is easier.

Then Emma wants to try the game lying on our sides. Ooh, that's hard!

Charlotte suggests trying it face-to-face with a partner. That's funny!

Instead of a five-minute warm-up activity, this game absorbs the entire half hour of music time. Pryce has led the way, and the children's creative collaboration, regardless of their differing needs, is too purposeful and fun to stop.

2025 Author's Note: Pryce is twenty-nine. He earned undergraduate (magna cum laude) and graduate degrees in computer science from Georgetown University in Washington, DC. He now lives with his partner in Bethesda, MD, and is a software engineer at the health information tech company Datavant. His mother comments, "He is very social and has time to catch up with friends and classmates and enjoys bar trivia and pub events. He has always been such an amazing, even-keeled, and wonderful son."

Pryce Bevan and his partner, Jessamine Griewahn-Okita

CONDUCTS on His Xylophone

(Originally published in *Autism Digest*, November 2019-January 2020. To protect his privacy, the child's name has been changed.)

For his first year, baby Daniel existed in an over-crowded, under-staffed Eastern European orphanage. Swaddled, he lay supine in a crib, staring at the ceiling. He was lifted out only to be fed or cleaned. Touching and being touched, moving and being moved were not part of his everyday experience. In this environment, Daniel was deprived of regular skin-on-skin contact, cuddling, and cooing that every baby requires to develop basic skills and especially emotional connections.

When his adoptive American parents brought him home, they noticed that he mostly sat and rarely cried. He had learned in the institution that crying was useless; no one heard, so no one came.

Not Yet Much of a Do-er

Three years later, preschooler Daniel was a watcher and not much of a do-er at St. Columba's Nursery School in Washington, DC. The screening for signs of SPD indicated that Daniel's tactile, vestibular, and proprioceptive systems were lagging, so we suggested that he get occupational therapy using sensory integration techniques (OT-SI) to help him participate and communicate more easily at school.

A sensory lifestyle at home and enticing sensory-motor activities at school helped this reticent child begin to move and participate more. However, while his motor coordination showed improvement, Daniel's language skills were uneven. His receptive language was excellent; he understood everything he heard, and he could read. But his expressive language was greatly delayed. He barely talked.

> **Receptive language:** The ability to understand how words express ideas and feelings. It is the language that one takes in by listening and reading. Expressive language is the spoken or written words and phrases that one puts out to communicate feelings and thoughts to others. Over-responsivity to touch, sounds, or movement may affect the child's ability to communicate effectively.

One way to communicate with a child who doesn't speak the way you do is to speak the way he does. What was Daniel's "language"?

Speaking and Singing in Numbers

Daniel spoke in numbers. On the playground, he would crouch at my feet and touch the grommets in my sneakers, one by one. He would point to the swings and sandbox buckets. "One, two, three ..." he'd whisper. He didn't choose to swing or dig, but if gently enticed, he might briefly allow his feet to leave the ground and his hands to get messy. Mostly, he counted objects, ignoring his classmates.

Daniel loved numbers, and he also loved music. In my music and movement room, he sat attentively on his blue felt "sit-upon," slightly outside the circle of other children. Touching and relating to kids was daunting, but responding to music was easy. He swayed and clapped to the beat, hummed the tunes, and learned some simple lyrics. His face glowed, his posture "zipped up," and his feedback made me feel like a fantastic teacher.

Number songs were his favorites. An example was the finger game "Fish Alive." Although Daniel lacked the fine-motor skills to articulate his fingers as nimbly as the other children, he enjoyed singing the numbers—and he always sang on pitch!

Holding up his fingers one by one in "Fish Alive" was hard for Daniel. He was better at using a mallet to strike the xylophone bars.

Fish Alive

Play:	C	D	E	F	G
Sing:	*1*	*2*	*3*	*4*	*5*
Extend:	Right Thumb	Index	Middle	Ring	Pinky
Play:	G	F	E	D	C
Sing:	*I*	*caught*	*a*	*fish*	*alive*
Move:	Bend forward and scoop an imaginary fish from the ocean.				
Play:	C	D	E	F	G
Sing:	*6*	*7*	*8*	*9*	*10*
Extend:	Left Thumb	Index	Middle	Ring	Pinky
Play:	G	F	E	D	C
Sing:	*I*	*let*	*it*	*swim*	*again*
Move:	Toss your imaginary fish back into the water.				

Therefore, a song he preferred was "Down, Down," which became "his song"—as long as he could stay seated.

"Down, Down" requires spinning. Spinning is fun for most children because they like to get dizzy. And falling is fun for most children because they know they can get up again. But spinning and falling are scary for a child with an immature vestibular system.

Down, Down

(Apply sticky numbers from 1 to 8 on the xylophone bars. This all-weather song starts an octave above Middle C on the piano, or on the 8th bar on the xylophone. For each verse, play the descending notes.)

Verse 1 — Play and sing:
8 - 7 - 6 - 5 - 4 - 3 - 2 - 1

Verse 2 — As fluttering leaves, you spin, fall, and sing:
Down, down, down, down, leaves are falling to the ground.

Verse 3 — As quiet snowflakes, tiptoe, swirl to the floor, and sing:
Down, down, down, down, snowflakes swirling to the ground.

Verse 4 — As louder raindrops, run quickly, drop, and sing:
Down, down, down, down, raindrops dropping to the ground.

Verse 5 — As noisy acorns, stomp, plop, and sing:
Down! down! down! down! Acorns plopping to the ground!

Daniel balked at first, so we made a deal: He would hold my hand and practice twirling like a leaf and falling to the ground. Two times, and then he could sit and be the accompanist. Clinging tightly, once, twice, he tentatively turned and inch by inch made his way to the floor. He was sweating, but he did it! Ta-da!

Conducting the Game on the Xylophone

Feeling good, Daniel picked up the xylophone and sat in the center of the rug. Then the magic began.

He became the conductor!

Imagine his playing the metal bars of the xylophone *with meaning*. His classmates perked up their ears. They heard what he was communicating and moved in response. He played softly; they swirled softly, like snow. He played quickly; they pattered around the room and fell quickly, like rain. He played staccato sounds; they plopped down hard on their bottoms, like acorns.

"Again, again!" the children cried. This was a new way of hearing a familiar tune, a new way of having *so much fun*. And so Daniel led his classmates, again and again, in a joyous game that they had learned to play together.

2025 Author's Note: "Daniel" attended St. Columba's Nursery School in Washington, DC, in the 1990s. I have lost touch with his family.

Sets the STAGE

(To be published in *Autism Digest* in 2025.)

Hannah Mitchell has made dramatic strides in her thirty-year life.

"Generally fearful" is how she describes herself in early childhood, growing up in Potomac, Maryland. She had an array of issues commonly besetting individuals with SPD, including auditory over-responsivity to loud noises and tactile over-responsivity to clothing textures. In addition, her vestibular system was out of sync; she had shaky balance, anxiety about moving upward on stairs or playground equipment, and poor awareness of where she was in space.

Selective Mutism

Hannah's fear of moving morphed into social anxiety. The specific form it took was selective mutism. Speaking to adults was especially hard for Hannah. She recalls one incident when she was in the backseat of her grandfather's car. She loved her "Pop Pop" and was mostly fine talking to him. However, she explains, "I wanted to say something to him, but the words wouldn't come out. I was so frustrated!"

> **Selective mutism:** A condition in which a person speaks easily in familiar situations—usually at home with family members—but is incapable of speaking in social scenarios, such as at school or when out and about. SPD can be an underlying reason for selective mutism when a child has difficulty processing sensations of sound, touch, and movement. Insecurity about one's own body and one's place in the world causes anxiety that often leads to shutting down and avoiding social interactions.

Play therapy with other children, medicine, and especially occupational therapy helped. (Hannah did not need speech-and-language therapy because she could express her thoughts and articulate her speech perfectly well at home.)

At her OT sessions, she remembers a great deal of swinging to strengthen her vestibular sense, and she loved swinging in her backyard too. Swinging is an activity that organizes the neurological system. It stimulates various brain parts and improves spatial awareness, rhythm, balance, muscle coordination, muscle strength, and mood. Furthermore, it promotes focus and attention.

Although her sibling was a bit envious ("Why does Hannah get OT and I don't?"), Hannah grew up in an understanding and nurturing family. They encouraged her to do everything she could and reassured her that nothing should ever limit her.

She says she was always a shy kid, but as a preteen, she grew more in sync with her world. Then, in high school, Hannah discovered theater. Interacting with teachers and other students was no longer a problem. She was elected vice-president of the Drama Club. She was more in tune with her body and voice. In her developing repertoire of skills were acting, singing, dancing—and (perhaps because of all that swinging?) organizing!

Organizational Skills

To her surprise, she says, "The high school drama teacher approached me because she thought I had the right skills to be the stage manager for an upcoming play in the fall. She especially appreciated my organizational skills." Hannah starred in this new role and volunteered to stage manage the bigger spring show. "I didn't know what I was doing, but the teacher helped, and I googled it and figured it out."

Then Hannah was off to Brandeis College, where she had a double major in psychology and theater. She intended to become a psychologist and help other anxious children. She did theater for fun, saying, "I loved being the person who collected all the information from everyone—actors, playwrights, directors, set designers, prop masters—and seeing that everyone got it. I loved making the director's vision come to life."

She was just a freshman, she says, when "a stage management professor noticed me and said I was really good at this. I became the go-to stage manager, and throughout college, I got to pick the shows I wanted to work on."

Stage-Managing in the Theater and Beyond

During the summertime, both during and after college, Hannah worked as an assistant stage manager at the Studio Theatre, which produces contemporary theater in intimate spaces to foster a more connected community. She also worked at the Williamstown Theater Festival in the Berkshires, which was then *the* place to meet New York theater people.

Her connections helped her get employed to stage-manage shows in off-Broadway venues, including The Public and MCC Theater, and do workshops for Broadway-bound shows. She also stage-managed the first national tour of the Broadway musical *Waitress* and worked on the stage management team for the International Emmy Awards.

Currently, Hannah has pivoted away from theater. She manages big events, such as a mile-long series of dance performances on New York City's High Line, a park built on a historic, elevated rail line where pedestrians can stroll through gardens, view art and sculpture, savor delicious food, and participate in live performances.

The sensory processing issues that constrained young Hannah no longer take center stage. She manages her own body and career while she guides others on how to act. Her advice to anyone in the audience? "Don't ever give up on anyone."

Hannah at the 2024 International Emmy Awards

stories about Individuals with Artistic & Technological Creativity

Spencer and Kori, with severe tactile over-responsivity as children, have grown up to be especially talented in using their hands. Among the many activities they participate in as adults, Kori works with animals and is a potter, and Spencer tinkers with tools and builds things such as his "multicopters."

REGARDING

Spencer Hamblin

★ ★ ★   ★ ★ ★

(Originally published in *Psychology Today*, March 2019.)

Spencer Hamblin and Carol Kranowitz, 2004

S pencer has always loved figuring things out. But at nine, he couldn't figure out how to "do school." He had to work hard to get through the school day because SPD and several other issues, including learning disabilities, got in his way.

His teacher could not, or would not, understand his out-of-sync behavior. She insisted, "He is so smart—he should know how to sit still, listen, and get his work done." She regarded Spencer as an unmotivated student and clumsy attention-getter—rather than a child who could shine if she would find the time to observe how his brain and body worked.

ISO a Children's Book about SPD

Spencer wanted to understand his sensory processing challenges. His mother, Nika, implored me to write a book to explain SPD in simple terms for children as well as for adults, such as Spencer's teacher, who could use a short course on the subject. *The Goodenoughs Get in Sync* was published in 2004 and reissued in 2023 as *The Out-of-Sync Family*. In the book, each family member has a different type of SPD. They experience a rough morning, help one another use their "sensory tools," and get in sync by evening.

When the book was published, I invited Nika and Spencer over to give them copies. Gingerbread cookies and lemonade, two foods that Nika said her picky eater especially liked, were on the table.

Spencer's Behavior: "Don't Regard Me"

Spencer sidled into the house. He did not look at me. He inched into the living room, reached for a gingerbread man, and slumped into a corner of the couch, watching warily as I sat down at the far end.

Nika and I chatted for a few minutes, and then I turned to regard Spencer, curled over his cookie. His body language was saying, "Don't touch me. Don't even look at me. Don't reproach me for slumping and being grumpy and not looking you in the eye. Just don't regard me at all."

His behavior was OK with me; I got it. Kids with special needs are often ill-at-ease in social situations. Because of certain observable issues—e.g., clumsy motor coordination, mumbled words, and limited eye contact—people often underestimate them. Meanwhile, their finely tuned feelings and deep interests go unobserved. Rebuffed by adults and other kids, these children find social contact to be just too daunting, so they withdraw. So would we all.

But each of us needs what the humanist psychologist Carl Rogers terms "unconditional positive regard." While everyone yearns to connect and be known, people like Spencer struggle to make those connections, especially with strangers.

I hoped to connect by showing my interest. I took a cookie, and we nibbled side by side for a moment. Then I asked, "Spencer, what do you like to think about?"

Spencer Turns On

Mid-nibble, Spencer froze. Slowly, he lowered his cookie, raised his eyes, and studied me. I must have passed the OK-vs.-Not-OK test, because he nodded and answered, "Batteries."

"Why batteries?"

"Because they can run the world efficiently and help save the environment."

A few more questions from me, and he was off and running. As if some magic hand had zipped up his spine, his posture changed, and he sat tall. Eyes aglow, he talked, smiled, and gestured for ten sparkling minutes about battery energy. He described how, in his plan, big batteries would not only empower cars, home appliances, cities, and space travel, but also clean up the planet.

He explained how these big batteries would be replenished by gigantic batteries.

I asked, "How will the gigantic batteries get *their* energy?"

"Solar power, I think." He sipped his lemonade. "I'm working on it." Then: "I wish you were my teacher." We smiled at each other while Nika wiped away a tear.

After more conversation, it was time for my guests to leave. Unprompted, Spencer gave me a bear hug and said, "Thank you. This was nice."

Wow!

Spencer has grown up. With his parents and a few teachers advocating for him, he has excelled at school. Always curious about how things work, he has become an electronics expert—building drones, leading a 4H Inventors' Group, and competing in national robotics competitions. At college he majors in electrical engineering and anticipates helping the world to become more energy efficient. He is one of my heroes.

In our interaction long ago, I was able to get in sync with Spencer because I had found that connecting with children with special needs takes extra thought, time, and empathy. Kids like Spencer are just like all children, only more so: they need to feel certain that they are safe, and heard, and known. They will let us in on their amazing thoughts and ardent feelings when our quiet, patient, special regard invests them with power.

★★ Spencer ★★
FIGURES It Out

(Excerpted from an article originally published in *Autism Asperger's Sensory Digest*, November 2021-January 2022, continuing Spencer's story.)

Spencer's sensory processing challenges were caused by Lyme disease. (In addition to having sensory issues, children with tick-borne diseases also may be non-verbal and are sometimes diagnosed with autism.) When he was eighteen, his parents switched him to an adult medical doctor—"much better than the pediatrician" who had missed Spencer's symptoms. When the correct diagnosis was made and treatment began, the sensory problems diminished.

Finding His Footing at School

At school, "Finding my footing took a while," Spencer says. Elementary school was rocky until his parents and a few teachers advocated for a meaningful IEP and other accommodations. In middle school, Spencer enrolled in a gifted/talented program where he had wonderful teachers. That change, he says, "went a long way."

With his medical problems finally under control, Spencer went to Frostburg State University in Maryland, where he worked on autonomous car research involving long-range sensors. With a major in electrical engineering and a minor in computer science, in 2021 he earned his BS with honors.

Solving Personal and Technical Problems

Spencer has grown to be an engaged, productive, and healthy adult. His tactile and other sensory challenges are minor. "I've gotten lucky," he says. "I can ignore them, or they just don't bother me." He has solved the problem of irritating food textures by becoming the family cook!

Still "obsessed with technology and anything mechanical or electronic," he intends to find the job of his dreams as an embedded hardware engineer. Spencer anticipates helping the world become more energy efficient, and we can be sure that he will figure it out.

One of Spencer's "Multicopters" before drone-building kits were available

Spencer at a STEM event at Northrop Grumman in Germantown, Maryland, 2014, with his "Multicopter" built from scratch

Displaying his creations at a New York MakerFaire, 2014

Spencer's hybrid Honda with a big battery

2025 Author's Note: After college graduation in 2021, Spencer found a job in industrial electrical equipment design. The hardware he designs is used to test spacecraft. He says, "My current job is extremely detail oriented, and my perfectionist streak has been very helpful. The difficult part is knowing when to turn it off and let it go. I've gotten better at this."

He lives with his parents in Silver Spring, Maryland, helping out with household tasks, especially in the kitchen. He says, "I used to really struggle with sensory issues and new foods. I was dangerously close to being one of those kids who only ate hot dogs and chicken nuggets. With time and effort, I've managed to overcome this issue. The biggest help was when I started cooking for myself in college. I controlled how new or different the food was, and I was able to explore new dishes at my own pace. Something about making it myself helped calm my nerves and helped me try new things."

He no longer has tactile issues, although he will never like the feel of tags on shirts. He still struggles with staying focused and avoiding distractions. The biggest challenge is tuning out nearby voices that make it nearly impossible to concentrate. He says, "I've fallen in love with noise-canceling headphones, which have been a massive help."

Outside of work, Spencer has gotten involved with a local Maker Group, a commercial capability-building firm. He says, "It can be hard to find people that I vibe with. I'm lucky to have found a group of like-minded individuals. Social connections are still something I struggle with. I find I get along best with others who are neurodivergent. It's happened multiple times where I click with someone and find out later on that they are dyslexic or have ADHD. It's happened too many times to ignore."

It seems fitting that Spencer's hobbies are collecting and restoring mechanical calculators. He also enjoys woodworking and hopes "to make a side gig out of it one day." And he now owns a beautiful blue hybrid car with a great big battery.

Considering where he stands today, he says, "Frankly, I am very lucky"—as is the world for having individuals like Spencer in it.

⋅⋅★ Kori Cotteleer ★⋅⋅

Throws POTS (Not Tantrums)

(To be published in *Autism Digest* in 2026.)

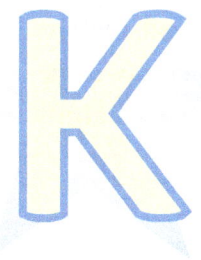

ori Cotteleer's childhood tactile issues governed everything she did. (Read her story in *The Out-of-Sync Child Grows Up*.) At home, for example, she threw tantrums over getting dressed. She stripped because she couldn't bear to wear clothes. Naked, she tried to sleep standing up to avoid touching bedsheets.

At school, tactile over-responsivity dictated that she couldn't handle crayons and scissors. She couldn't wash her hands because the soap was "icky" and the paper towels were "wrong." She couldn't interact with classmates. She spent kindergarten under the table—but her teacher didn't realize Kori had sensory issues and wouldn't have known how to help.

Indeed, nobody knew how to help until Kori's parents learned about SPD and—literally—got the ball rolling.

What Helped

Today, Kori, thirty-two, is a confident, gregarious, cheerful young woman. Among the many reasons she has developed so positively are:

- Family support (understanding and accommodating her sensory needs with home activities such as rolling a therapy ball over her and having pillow fights);
- Intense OT-SI (intense tactile and proprioceptive input such as jumping into ball pits and receiving lots of deep pressure to her skin and muscles); and
- Stout-heartedness (her determination to wear clothes and jeans, like other kids, and to ride a horse).

Tactile over-responsivity no longer rules Kori's life. True, some general anxiety—the bane of everyone with SPD—still lingers, but she now knows how to manage it. The fabric of clothes still matters. Sometimes wearing something tight is just right; sometimes something loose is best. She still sleeps in her father's big, worn T-shirts.

Work, Love, and Pots

Socially, interacting with other people is now a pleasure. Kori's occupation is as a full-time manager at a large veterinarian clinic with seven doctors. She manages the technicians and assistants and works with animals all day. It is messy work, and she loves it.

The little girl with a severe tactile problem grew up to become "very much a hugger." These days, she likes being touched and says with a laugh, "Cuddling works really well." In 2025 she married Connor Kern, a "wonderful man." Their wedding took place at a nature center with a snapping turtle, eagle, and owl presiding at the reception. At home in Kenosha, Wisconsin, they live with a lizard, a snake, and three "loving, needy, but *great* cats."

In addition, the child who couldn't touch icky soap in the school bathroom grew up to become—get this—a potter! After two years of potting classes, she has mastered the art. With a laugh, she says, "These days I throw pots, not tantrums!"

"When Connor and I talked about moving in together," she says, "he told me I could take over the basement and put in my own wheel and kiln. I said, 'I'm sold!'"

She goes on, "He totally gets me. When I'm stressed, he tells me to go make pots. I get mentally and physically connected to the whole potting process. I am fully immersed. It's like playing with shaving cream with my OT when I was little. I come back upstairs covered in clay and take a hot bath, and then I am calm."

She makes vases for friends' weddings and sells pots at a plant store and also online. She and Connor, who enjoys woodworking in his spare time, frequently sell their wares at craft shows. (See her work at www.instagram.com/clay_with_kori/.)

What Folks Should Know

Asked what she wants folks to know, Kori answers, "I want people to be OK with how their sensory challenges make them feel. They should understand that comfort is way more important than style. Wear what makes you feel OK."

She continues, "And people shouldn't feel guilty or ashamed about their sensory issues. When you're having a meltdown, you're in survival mode. It's a crisis. You're trying to get through that terrible minute. You need understanding and support.

"When I would have a breakdown and couldn't get dressed, it impacted the family, because everyone had to stay home. I took up so much time and energy. But my mom made my SPD a family thing. She made it OK. My siblings don't resent all the attention and the OT I got. I love them so much and am so grateful."

Our conversation has taken place on Kori's day off when she is babysitting for her little nephew. The next thing on the day's agenda is to roll a ball back and forth with him and then—what else?—go throw a pot.

Kori with one of her pots

Kori gets a cow kiss

Connor Kern and Kori at a craft show

stories about Individuals with Fix-It-Ability

Individuals with SPD know well how uncomfortable a noisy, crowded, hot environment can be. Todd, David, and Rebecca put their efforts into making the world more livable for all people.

⋅⋆★ Todd Root ★⋆⋅

PLUGS In

(Originally published in *Autism Digest*, February-April 2025.)

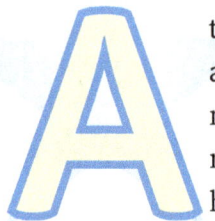

t seven, Todd Root's "100 percent logic-based brain" and synergetic thinking were in full bloom. He loved math, visualizing it in glorious color and complex networks. But because his verbal skills didn't match his math skills, he couldn't explain how the colors and hues revealed a solution.

Alas, his teachers had zero understanding of his autistic brain and extrasensory gifts. They would say, "Show us how you do it. Just write it out on the board." He would say, "That's not how I do it!"

Not getting how he got it, they implied he must be cheating. They denied him his fidgets. Then they decided he needed tutoring … during recess!

Lost Opportunities to Move and Play

Keeping him indoors to do math their way deprived him of opportunities to move and play freely outdoors with his classmates. Todd remembers, "They were nice ladies and probably good teachers, doing their best with the knowledge they had at the time. But they shortchanged my social development, because they weren't plugging me in to experiences to learn and grow in a communicative way."

School experiences like this were the basis of Todd's lifelong interest in figuring out how to succeed in life without being forced to jump through other people's hoops. He determined that if others weren't plugged into him, he would attempt to plug into them. He took notes of others' behavior and learned to emulate it, seemingly doing a great job with his actions, reactions, and interactions.

Todd's Books of "Maps"

One self-help tool Todd began using in tenth grade is his book of tips, or maps, which is always by his side. In each book—currently his ninety-fourth—he jots down best practices that he borrows to meet the challenges of daily scenarios in personal and professional life.

A map may be about the etiquette of getting a slice of pizza when among a hungry group. It may structure how to deliver a presentation, handle a disagreement, stay in a crowded room when he is on sensory overload, or manage "small talk and tall talk." These books have increased self-awareness as he acknowledges his challenges and creates frameworks for success. His books also honor great mentors who have said, "Look at what Todd brings. What can't he do? What's on his horizon? Let's make it happen!"

Todd made a lot happen when he brought his math wizardry to the financial world in New York's Wall Street and in San Francisco. With his small books at hand to map the way, he excelled in complex and ultra-fast-paced interactions involving vast amounts of global wealth ... but he "just did it" without feeling really attached to that line of work.

Making School Better

Always, the educational world has been his interest. He especially enjoys making school better for students who think differently from typical kids. He also enjoys helping educators, professionals, and parents understand sensory differences, neurodivergent learning, and non-traditional teaching approaches. Gratification comes when he helps neurotypical individuals "discover how effective they can be when they can see a subject at the micro-granular level, but they can't do that if they're not totally plugged in!"

Todd says, "Kids need to plug themselves in to learn how the world works and to look ahead." His aim to guide students and educators intensified when his daughter, at four, was diagnosed with a form of autism formerly called *pervasive developmental disorder not otherwise specified* (PDD-NOS). This condition impaired her ability to regulate sensory experiences and affected her behavior, social interactions, and communication skills.

Todd determined to assist his little girl and other neurodivergent children so they would be comfortable, known, and equipped to succeed at school. With her empathetic parents' guidance, her teachers' growing understanding, and her innate gifts, Todd's daughter flourished at school and beyond.

Todd has made good things happen as director of Donor Advisory at the Independence Academy of Indiana, a school for neurodivergent children in third through twelfth grades. He raises awareness of the school and also raises money, helping donors make dreams come to fruition. For example, the school recently moved to a two-acre campus with space for a sensational playground. One problem with the site, however, is its location beside a highway and a nearby airport.

Todd was sensitive to the visual and auditory stimulation affecting the children as they arrived at school. He intuited what drama might have gone on earlier at home that increased the anxiety of students, many of whom he knew started their day under stressful conditions. The din from the road and sky didn't help.

An Acoustic Wall Made with Trees

In sync with the kids' emotional state, he came up with the solution of building an acoustic wall. He learned about a nonprofit organization, Keep Indianapolis Beautiful (KIB), whose mission is to engage diverse communities to create vibrant public places, helping people and nature thrive. He contacted Jeremy Kranowitz (Carol's son), KIB's president and CEO, and made a proposal. Together, they found a donor enthusiastic about funding a tree-planting project.

In 2023, volunteers from KIB, the fire department, PNC Bank, and friendly corporations, alongside students and teachers, planted forty trees that border the schoolyard and dim the racket coming from the cars and planes. The trees have made the schoolyard beautiful in the traditional way—and even more beautiful for people who need it in another way. Now, the trees are an attractive and soothing part of the children's tree-tending work and daily activity walks around the school.

Where will Todd Root plug in next? The world of publishing! His big book, *Jumping through Hoops: Perspectives from Being Autistic in a World of Neurotypical People*, will be issued in 2025. It will present how autism affects him and how his map of the world may positively affect others in order to bring about understanding, remove barriers, and help people map their own pathways in life.

2025 Author's Note: Todd has moved on to an exciting job as president of Building Essential Skills Together (BEST), a nonprofit that provides purposeful and meaningful opportunities to individuals of *all* abilities through supported life and job skills development (www.buildingessentialskills.org).

Todd is also a clinical advisory board member for Cicero Therapies and their clinics in the Midwest and on the East Coast. This organization offers comprehensive, collaborative, and compassionate care for all children and families (www.cicerotherapies.com).

Uses His SPD to Design Better Buildings

(Originally published in *Autism Digest*, November 2023-January 2024.)

Everyone else wore a shirt—but not David!

A s a child, David Bainbridge believed that no one could possibly like shirts, so why did all the other kids wear them? He wondered how other children endured—and apparently enjoyed—bright, noisy birthday parties. He saw that his brother loved amusement parks, easily remembered what was said to him, and could eat anything, so why couldn't David do those things too?

A "Too Much Kid"

David was a "too much kid" (a term coined by Carrie Fannin, an SPD mom and executive director of the Children's Institute for Learning Differences in Washington state). David was perpetually, perplexingly overwhelmed with sensations of sound, sight, smell, touch, and movement. His lifetime challenge has been sensory over-responsivity, but nobody recognized that problem while he was growing up.

With his wide interests, David considered various careers as he matured. He wanted to be an oceanographer ... but got seasick in a rowboat. He decided to become an environmental planner ... but couldn't tolerate sitting still in confined spaces during lengthy meetings. He was keen on studying people's habitats around the world ... but found that traveling through loud, chaotic airports was hellish. His paradise was the desert or the lake, alone.

"If you like to work alone," David says, "SPD is OK. However, it would have helped if I had recognized SPD earlier in my life." Throughout his childhood and adulthood, he did not understand why he was hyper-sensitive to ordinary sounds or had panic attacks in crowds. The physical and emotional cost of this mystery was high.

David Bainbridge in one of his favorite environments

Careers to Fit Neurological Needs

Through trial and error, David, now in his seventies, has learned to select career options that fit his neurological needs, such as working outdoors or doing library research. Over his fifty-year career, he spent just a few months working inside buildings with noisy heating and cooling systems, bad lighting, noxious smells, and poor air quality. Those physically painful months were enough to launch him into his life work: analyzing the environmental impact of unhealthy buildings on employees.

David knew he was different but did not know about SPD until he was sixty-eight. Always interested in building design, he was curious about Temple Grandin's humane animal-treatment facilities. He picked up her book, *The Autistic Brain: Helping Different*

Kinds of Minds Succeed, read about the sensory challenges of cattle and many people, and had an epiphany.

"SPD—that's me!" He went on to read other books about sensory challenges, and at last, David understood his own biology, preferences, and personality. He has learned that one can shape one's career path to what one's brain can do. "I discovered SPD as the experience of my world. It's comforting to know what forces are in play. SPD is partly the reason that I have done those things that make me happy."

Healthy, Safe, and Comfortable Buildings

Today, at his solar research and design firm, Living Systems, in San Diego, David uses his knowledge about SPD to make buildings better. He focuses on community design, passive solar heating and cooling, building codes, and solar rights. His latest publication is *Accountability: Why We Need to Count Social and Environmental Cost for a Livable Future*. The book explains the "true cost" of poorly designed buildings. It urges architects, construction companies, civic leaders, and the population at large to insist on buildings that keep us all healthy, safe, and comfortable. (Read about his amazing work at https://works.bepress.com/david_a_bainbridge/.)

What would our world be like without neurodivergent thinkers like David Bainbridge?

⋆⋆★ **Rebecca Spring** ★⋆⋆

COOLS the World

(Originally published in *Autism Digest*, May-July 2025.)

Reb Spring with the bullhorn: "Our Home Is On Fire"

Like many people with SPD and mild, undiagnosed autism, nineteen-year-old Rebecca—or Reb—Spring is challenged in several sensory realms. She has auditory over-responsiveness to loud sounds, for example. "At school the other day, I jumped out of my skin when a fire alarm went off. It was a visceral reaction."

Her over-responsive gustatory sense affects which tastes she can tolerate.

And her tactile over-responsivity is the biggie. Only certain soft textures in clothing are tolerable, and she never wears jeans. The textures (as well as the tastes) of food determine what she eats. "There's a narrow range of foods I like," she says. "I still separate food on the plate and pick out items that I don't want to eat, but I have expanded and am more flexible now."

Interoceptive Sensation of Feeling Hot

What bothers Reb most of all is the interoceptive sensation of feeling hot. Her mother, Carol Foltz Spring, recalls, "She was a newborn in the winter, and when we went out, she would rip off her hat. Older women in the neighborhood would scold me for bringing my baby outside without a hat. She always ran hot!"

> **Interoception:** An internal sensory system, helps to regulate and make us aware of body functions inside our body, such as temperature, heart rate, thirst, and hunger.

"I definitely have issues with strong heat," Reb says. "When I was growing up in Washington, DC, we had no air conditioning at home. Summers were painful. It was hard to go to sleep." As a child, she began to ponder how heat affects people's thinking and behavior— and about what she could do to fix the problem.

Becoming a Climate Activist

Today, Reb is finishing her first college year at The New School in New York City where she majors in environmental studies. In line with her coursework, she is a climate activist, advocating for decreasing fossil fuel consumption, CO_2, and methane emissions. Reb has organized several marches, where she, her classmates, and other like-minded individuals block the entrances to prominent banks such as CitiBank and investment firms that are big funders of fossil fuels. She wants people who have pension funds to urge their banks to invest in sustainable fuel and to move their money to other banks that sponsor socially responsible energy such as electrification.

"Protesting gives me a lot of energy," she says. "I'm passionate about it. Sometimes it's stressful, especially when police are aggressive, when they're pushing and shoving and yelling at us to get out of the way. I'm a conflict avoider, and the sensory aspect of all that touching is really hard."

Prepping for Creativity

To alleviate that stress, Reb does a little stimming. She runs around in circles and does hand motions, "all in a good way. The action stimulates me and gets me into a space where I can be creative." This kind of movement, which Reb calls "pretending," helps her process real life and imagine scenarios where she may someday find herself.

> **Stimming:** Self-stimulating, repetitive body movements or vocalizations. Many individuals with autism and other neurodevelopmental conditions engage in this kind of behavior. It is a coping mechanism that helps them feel calm and able to express their feelings.

Excerpted from *A Love Letter to the Parks*, by Rebecca Spring

A month ago, I remember lying down in Prospect Park

The soft grass tickles my elbow

Laughs fill the cool autumn air

Vendors roam selling sticky sweet treats

My friends and I teach each other games as we sit back with full bellies

The trees whisper all around

Something is coming

But we didn't hear them

Growling flames burst into the air in Prospect Park

Sparks and ash float then fall

As ancient trees are burnt down to debris on the rough pavement below

Forest fires in New York City

Once a tale of dystopian novels, today a reality

The New York Post blames vagrants

But we know the real culprit: climate change

Who's going to defend the trees?

Drought now has a chokehold grip on our home

Forest fires burn in our cities, orange smoke filling the air

Ecosystems chopped down for the profit of a few

What can we do?

A war is raging on Earth, but we must resist!

Fighting back, our spirits lift

Direct action is our guiding light

That's our hope to make things right

Another stress reliever is dancing. She says, "I like getting into the rhythm of it. I feel the music and get into my own space, where I can let loose and improvise." Pausing, this seemingly reserved young woman laughs and says, "People tell me I'm a wild dancer."

"Pretending" and dancing prepare Reb to tap into her feelings in various ways. She has composed music for violin and piano and has written short stories, a novel, and poems. "I've written poetry about climate and social issues, and also about my personal life, particularly about how it feels when people don't respect my boundaries. Writing sensory descriptions is powerful and very important to me."

What does Reb foresee herself doing after college? She intends to continue environmental activism and creative writing while honing skills in documentary filmmaking. All the pieces fit together as Reb, with extrasensory grace, puts to use her hot zeal for a cooler world.

Beating the drum to "Fund Education, Not Genocide

Demanding debt cancellation from the International Monetary Fund

Advocating for Climate Justice

Protesting Washington Gas's expansion of toxic methane gas in DC

Photo by Doug Bolst

Carol Stock Kranowitz observed many children with sensory processing differences (SPD) and mild autism during her twenty-five-year career as a preschool teacher. To help them become more competent in their work and play, she studied sensory processing and sensory integration (SI) theory. She learned to help identify her young students' needs and to steer them into early intervention. Today, she writes and speaks about SPD's effect on children's learning and behavior and how families, teachers, therapists, and other professionals can support children as they grow.

Since its publication in 1998, the first book in her Sync series, *The Out-of-Sync Child*, has become one of the most popular books about sensory processing and related issues. Her books have been translated into twenty-one languages and have sold more than a million copies.

A graduate of Barnard College of Columbia University, Carol has a master's degree in education and human development from George Washington University. She lives in Maryland, plays the cello, and dotes on five sensational grandchildren.

Carol's materials for parents, teachers, professionals, and children include the following:

Out-of-Sync Child Books

The Out-of-Sync Child: Recognizing and Coping with Sensory Processing Differences, 3rd ed. (2022). New York: TarcherPerigee. Also available in an audio version. New York: TarcherPerigee.

The Out-of-Sync Child Has Fun: Activities for Kids with SPD, 2nd ed. (2006). Perigee.

The Out-of-Sync Child Grows Up: Coping with Sensory Processing Disorder in the Adolescent and Young Adult Years (2016). TarcherPerigee.

Children's Books

The Out-of-Sync Family: A Story about Sensory Differences (2023). Arlington, TX: Sensory World.

Good Times with Out-of-Sync Grandkids: Activities for Grown-ups and Children with Sensory Processing Differences (2025). Arlington, TX: Sensory World.

Absolutely No Dogs Allowed! (2015). Alphabet book by Asher Kranowitz, with Carol's guidelines for discussing senses and emotions with children. Arlington, TX: Sensory World.

101 Activities for Kids in Tight Spaces (1995). New York: St. Martin's.

About the Author and Her Books

Screening Manuals for Teachers and Therapists

Preschool SENsory Scan for Educators, or Preschool SENSE (2006). Arlington, TX: Sensory Resources.

Balzer-Martin Preschool Screening Program Manual, with Lynn Balzer-Martin (1987). Washington, DC: St. Columba's Nursery School.

Answers to Questions Teachers Ask about Sensory Integration, 3rd ed., with Jane Koomar, Stacey Szklut, et al. (2014). Arlington, TX: Sensory World.

In-Sync Child Publications with Joye Newman

Growing an In-Sync Child: Simple, Fun Activities to Help Every Child Develop, Learn and Grow. (2010). Perigee.

In-Sync Activity Cards: 50 Simple, New Activities to Help Children Develop, Learn, and Grow (2012). Sensory World. Also published as *The In-Sync Activity Card Book* (2015), Sensory World; and in digital format in English, French, Greek, Italian, and Spanish (2021), www.upbility.net.

The In-Sync Child Program webinars (2021). Ten-part series about child development and fun activities. In English at www.insyncchild.com/. In French, Greek, Italian, and Spanish (2021) at www.upbility.net.

A Year of Mini-Moves for the In-Sync Child (2021). Weekly schedules in digital format, in English, French, Greek, Italian, and Spanish at www.upbility.net. In English hardcopy at Sensory World.

To learn more, visit **www.out-of-sync-child.com** and **www.insyncchild.com**.

Did you like this book?

Rate it and share your opinion!

Not what you expected? Tell us!

Most negative reviews occur when the book did not reach expectation. Did the description build any expectations that were not met? Let us know how we can do better.

Please drop us a line at info@fhautism.com.
Thank you so much for your support!

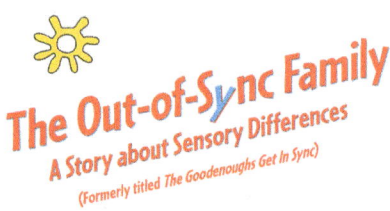

from Sensory World

with Joye Newman

by Asher Kranowitz

Sensory World
A proud imprint of Future Horizons

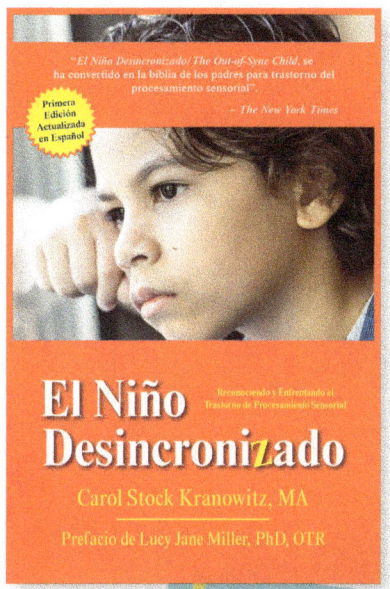

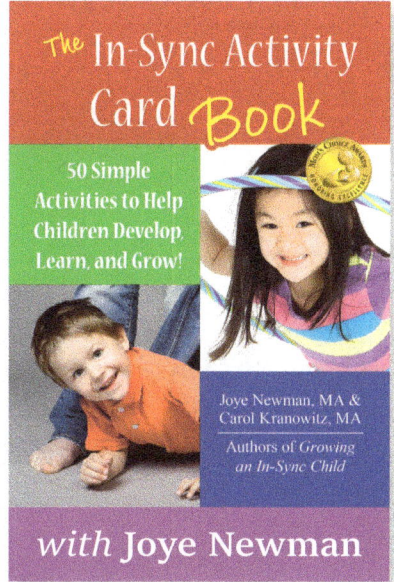

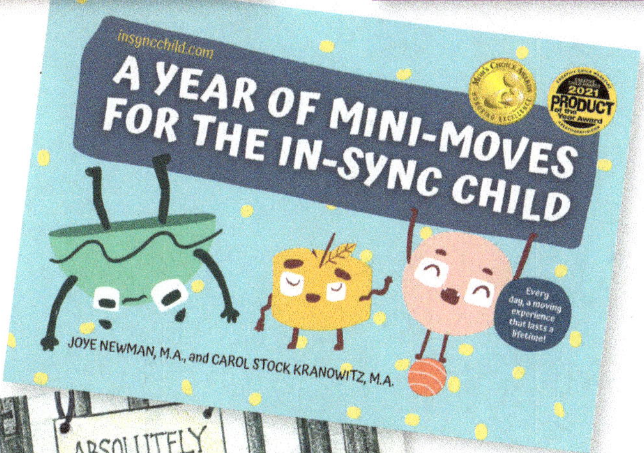

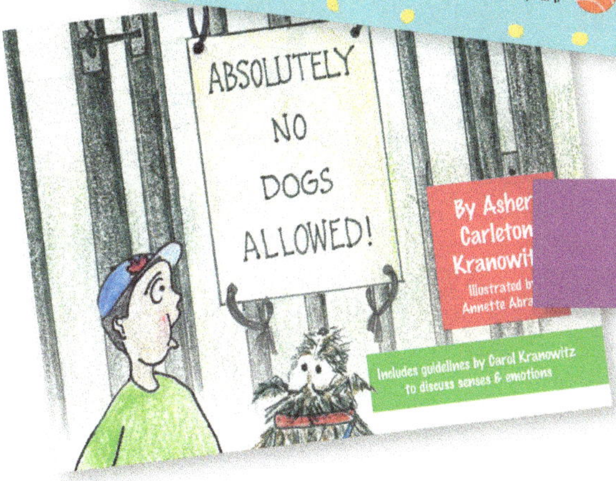

www.ingramcontent.com/pod-product-compliance
Lightning Source LLC
Jackson TN
JSHW080833200725
87896JS00003B/3